# Jewish History
# The BIG Picture

## LEADER'S GUIDE

by Ellen J. Rank

Behrman House Publishers
www.behrmanhouse.com

# CONTENTS



*Editor*: Dena Neusner
*Production Manager*: Jessica Gurtman

Springfield, New Jersey
www.behrmanhouse.com

ISBN: 978-0-87441-837-8
Manufactured in the United States of America

**Part Three: Enlightenment and Emancipation**



**Part Four: Antisemitism and Zionism**



**Part Five: Devastation and Rebirth**

# INTRODUCTION

## Jewish History: The BIG Picture

This leader's guide is designed to be used in conjunction with *Jewish History: The Big Picture*, by Gila Gevirtz, for an adult education class in Jewish history.

Deborah E. Lipstadt asks in the foreword, "What will we do with the history we study?" As teachers, we want people to learn from the past, to understand how their actions are affected by their history, and to think about how they can help shape the future of Judaism, the Jewish community, and the world. The more we learn, the more we are able to ask our own questions, such as:

"What is history's relevance to me?"

"How can history guide me in how to live my life and be a positive force in my community and the world?"

There are three main themes woven into *Jewish History: The Big Picture*--

- The **adaptability** of the Jewish people
- The **diversity** of the Jewish people
- The **centrality** of the land of Israel to the Jewish people

Most of the questions in this leader's guide focus on these themes, to help us understand Judaism and the Jewish community throughout history.

# How to Use This Leader's Guide

*Jewish History: The Big Picture* is comprised of twenty-seven chapters organized into five main parts. This leader's guide follows the organization of the book, and consists of an overview of each chapter's contents, the core concepts for that chapter, and questions that will help stimulate discussion in a study group or class.

The discussion questions are presented in three ways:

- **BIG Picture Questions**—five overarching questions that relate to themes spanning the entire book
- **Chapter Questions**—two or three questions specific to each chapter
- **Part Overview Questions**—additional questions for each part of the book.

*Jewish History: The Big Picture* can be used as the core text for a variety of different types of classes or study groups, ranging in intensity and length. The following are some possibilities:

1. **Adult Education Class**: Ask participants to read two or three chapters for each meeting. Use the chapter questions to stimulate discussion.
2. **Shabbat Study Group**: Organize a monthly Shabbat study group, perhaps meeting after services. Ask participants to read one part of the book in preparation for each meeting. Use the part overview questions to enhance your discussions.
3. **Book Club**: Choose *Jewish History: The Big Picture* as a selection for a book club. Use the big picture questions to stimulate discussion.
4. ***Leil Tikkun*, Night of Study**: Encourage congregants to read *Jewish History: The Big Picture* prior to Shavuot. Use the big picture questions to guide your discussions.
5. **Community Project:** Schedule a study session on Part One of the book as a kickoff for a community project. Meet monthly, studying one part each month. Inspire a deeper commitment to fundraising and community building as participants' affirmation as Jews is strengthened by this new knowledge.
6. **Professional Development**: Use *Jewish History: The BIG Picture* for in-service professional development for religious school teachers. Devote part of each staff meeting to a discussion based on a chapter or section of the book.

We hope that this leader's guide will serve as a springboard for lively, informative, and reflective discussions.

# Community Projects

You may also wish to design a family- or community-based project that can help participants personalize their understanding of Jewish history and deepen their ties to their community. Some possibilities are:

1. **Personalized Timelines**

   Invite participants to create timelines incorporating both key events in Jewish history and important events in the lives of their families, such as their great-grandparents' weddings, the date that their family immigrated to America, or the birthdates of their children. Community events, such as the founding of their synagogue or Jewish community center, could also be included. Encourage participants to enhance their timelines with copies of relevant photographs and documents. You may choose to display these timelines in a main hall of the synagogue or JCC.

2. **Family Stories and Histories**

   Encourage participants to write down or record stories from their family history, based on their own memories, interviews with other family members, and relevant documents. Combine these stories with family photographs and documents to create a presentation of each participant's family history. Hold a special program for synagogue and community members to come and view this personalized telling of Jewish history.

3. **Teaching Jewish History with Maps**

   Display a large map of the world on a wall or bulletin board. Ask each participant to show the journeys of his or her family by using thread to connect the places their family has lived. For example, one person may affix three pieces of purple thread: one from Kiev, Ukraine, to Newark, New Jersey, for a maternal grandparent; one from Austria to London, England, to Cincinnati, Ohio, for a maternal grandparent; and one from Łódź, Poland, to Los Angeles, California, for both paternal grandparents. Display the map in a public place in the synagogue, along with a list of the participants and a description of each of their family's journeys.

# BIG PICTURE QUESTIONS

These overview questions relate to themes found throughout *Jewish History: The Big Picture,* and can guide your discussions about the book as a whole.

1. **Identity:** How have the Jewish people kept their Jewish identity strong for more than two thousand years while living in diverse communities around the world? Looking forward, what kinds of choices and decisions will Jews need to make in the future, in order to preserve the vitality of Judaism and the Jewish community?

2. **Diversity:** What are some of the different beliefs and values that caused the Jewish people to branch out into diverse groups such as the Reform, Conservative, Reconstructionist, and Orthodox movements? What are the unifying values, beliefs, and ideals that are inherent to Judaism and shared by all practicing Jews? How might various Jewish groups bond together and see themselves truly as one nation?

3. **Social Justice:** How has the core Jewish value of social justice motivated Jews to work toward building a better world? What forces help make a person willing to take risks or make sacrifices for the sake of a greater or common good? How can we help motivate and prepare the next generation of Jews to actively pursue social justice?

4. **Israel:** What kinds of connections did Jews maintain with the land of Israel for the thousands of years that Israel was ruled by others? How was the Jewish community changed by the destruction of the Second Temple and by the establishment of the State of Israel? What can be done to help Diaspora Jews maintain a relationship with Israel, and how might this help to keep Judaism and the Jewish community strong?

5. **Demographics:** How and why has the demography of the Jewish people changed since World War II? What are the positive and negative effects of Judaism having changed from a truly worldwide religion to a religion centered in a few of the world's wealthiest and most advanced countries? How might these demographic changes affect the continued vitality of Judaism and the Jewish community?

# PART ONE: ORIGINS AND EXILE

Early Israelites kept Judaism alive under different types of rule: as a group of tribes; as a unified, self-governed people; as exiles from their homeland; and as subjects in their homeland to foreign rulers.

## Introduction

*...book pages 6-8*

*The Birth of the Jewish People and Monotheism*

### Chapter Overview

The early Israelites distinguished themselves by their monotheistic beliefs—the belief in a single God—in contrast to their neighbors, who believed in and prayed to many gods.

### Core Concepts

- Monotheism fostered the Israelites' development of a strong ethical code.
- Today, Jews are guided by the same core ethical values as their ancestors.

### Discussion Questions

1. How do the historical and biblical accounts provide us with different insights into the Jewish experience? In what ways are they complementary?

2. What values and beliefs separated the ancient Israelites from their neighbors? Do you feel that any of your values and/or beliefs separate you from your neighbors?

# Chapter 1: The Early Israelites

***...book pages 9-16***

## *Adapting to a Changing World*

### Chapter Overview

Israel became a unified kingdom under King David, but later it split in two and eventually was destroyed. Many Israelites were forced out of their homeland, yet some returned to rebuild it, even as others remained in the Diaspora to flourish in foreign lands. Many Jews who lived in Israel and in the Diaspora were able to adapt Judaism to their changing circumstances.

### Core Concepts

- As their circumstances changed, the Israelites changed their way of life in order to adapt to the loss of their Temple, their land, and their leaders.
- Despite the many adaptations they made, both in the land of Israel and in exile, the Israelites maintained their core religious beliefs and identities.
- The Israelites' ability to adapt can serve today's Jews as a model for balancing the need for change with a commitment to Jewish tradition.

**Words to Know**
*Diaspora*: p.14. Places outside the Land of Israel where Jews live.

### Discussion Questions

1. How did the Israelites' values and beliefs help them to maintain their Jewish identity when they had their own kingdom, as well as when they were under foreign rule? How do your values and beliefs help you to define your religious identity today?

2. What are some of the ways the Israelites adapted to their society without abandoning their core religious values? What are some of the ways that North American Jews today adapt to the society in which they live while at the same time maintaining their Jewish identity?

3. What motivated Persian Jews during the time of Ezra and Nehemiah to return to Israel? What factors motivate some modern Jews to make *aliyah* (immigrate to Israel)? Is making *aliyah* a Jewish imperative today?

# Chapter 2: The Age of Hellenism

***...book pages 17-24***

## *Strategies for Survival*

### Chapter Overview

The lure and force of Greek culture polarized the Jews of Israel. Jews responded to Hellenism with resistance, assimilation, and adaptation. For the most part, Diaspora Jews chose to adapt to Hellenism while maintaining their religious identity and their ties to the Jews of Judea. While the Judean Jews ultimately regained their independence under the Hasmoneans, they confronted great challenges due to the ongoing influence of Hellenism in the region.

### Core Concepts

- The Jews responded to the challenge of Hellenism with diverse strategies: resistance to Hellenization, complete assimilation, and varying levels of adaptation to Greek culture.
- Jews continue to use variations on these strategies in facing the challenges of our own time.

**Words to Know**
*Hellenism*: p.18. The integration of Greek culture into the local culture.

### Discussion Questions

1. Aḥad Ha'Am, a Zionist who lived from 1856 to 1927, once said, "More than Israel has kept the Sabbath, the Sabbath has kept Israel." How does this statement help us to understand why Antiochus chose to ban the observance of Shabbat?

2. What were some of the conflicts that arose among the Jewish people who disagreed on the best response to Hellenism (resistance, assimilation, or adaptation)? How do differing opinions about these same three responses to modern society cause conflicts and tensions among Jews today?

3. How can the varying responses of Jews from the "Age of Hellenism" serve as examples for Jews today in regard to resisting assimilation?

# Chapter 3: Roman Domination of Judea ***...book pages 25-36***

## *Divisions Inside and Out*

### Chapter Overview

The Jews of Judea were divided politically, economically, and religiously. Oppression by Roman rulers further complicated and aggravated the growing intolerance among the different groups of Jews. Ideally, the Jews would have united against their common enemy. Instead tensions between the diverse groups (e.g., Sadducees, Pharisees, Zealots, and Sicarii) led to civil conflicts and ultimately contributed to the destruction of the Second Temple.

### Core Concepts

- The Jews of Judea were diverse in their beliefs and practices.
- Their lack of tolerance and respect for one another brought the Jews to the verge of self-destruction, through civil war that blinded them to the more serious threat of the expanding Roman Empire.
- Jews today are still faced with the challenge of valuing what they have in common and respecting their differences.

### Discussion Questions

1. What were some of the ramifications of intolerance among the politically, economically, and religiously diverse Jews of Judea? What are some of the problems Jews face today due to lack of tolerance and understanding among the Jewish people?

2. What prevented the Jews of Judea from valuing each other's approach to Judaism and from working toward a shared vision? How might Jews today work toward greater understanding and tolerance of one another? What would be some of the benefits of learning to value one another's hopes and beliefs?

# Part One Overview Questions

*...book pages 5-36*

These questions may be used to guide your discussions about the entirety of **Part One: Origins and Exile** (chapters 1-3).

1. Early Israelites lived under different types of rule: as a group of tribes; as a unified, self-governed people; as exiles from their homeland; and as subjects in their homeland to foreign rulers. How did early Israelites adapt to these changes to maintain their Jewish identity? What were some of the challenges they faced during this time? What are some challenges faced today by North American Jews who wish to maintain their Jewish identity? How might Jews today respond to these challenges?

2. What caused intolerance and lack of understanding among the Jews of ancient Israel? Describe some of the ramifications of the tensions and conflicts among the groups. What are some conflicts today among Jews? What are some examples of different groups of Jews coming together for a common cause? How might Jews today learn to show one another greater respect and tolerance?

3. In what ways was the Land of Israel central to the Jewish people, both those living in the Land of Israel and those living in the Diaspora, from the birth of the Jewish people to the time of the destruction of the Second Temple? What are some of the ways that Israel is important today to Jews worldwide?

# PART TWO: DIASPORA AND DIVERSITY

After the destruction of the Second Temple, Jews reinvented their religion and met new challenges in the lands of the Diaspora.

## Chapter 4: Rabbinic Judaism

***...book pages 39-46***

*Reinventing a Religion and an Identity*

### Chapter Overview

After the destruction of the Second Temple, the center of Judaism shifted from the Temple to the Torah. The rabbis made key innovations during this period, including the founding of an academy in Yavneh where Torah scholars could learn, debate, and pass on Jewish teachings from one generation to the next. The rabbis also established a religious court that decided which books would be included in the Bible and formalized aspects of prayer. Prayer eventually replaced sacrifice as the central form of Jewish worship.

### Core Concepts

- The sages reoriented Judaism from a cult religion reliant upon the land of Israel, Jerusalem, and the Holy Temple to a religion that could survive and flourish after the destruction of the Temple and the exile of the Jews from the land of Israel.
- Jews today continue to renew the vision of Judaism so that it not only survives the challenges of today but also thrives.

### Discussion Questions

1. How did Yoḥanan ben Zakkai help shape Judaism to survive the loss of the Temple? How do Jews today call upon hope and innovation to address modern challenges? What challenges do the Jewish people still have to resolve?

2. How have today's Jewish traditions and customs been shaped by the early rabbis? How might rabbinic decisions of today influence Judaism for future generations?

# Chapter 5: Judaism and Christianity

***...book pages 47-56***

## *A Parting of the Ways*

### Chapter Overview

Infighting among the Jews, corruption among the Jewish religious leadership, and oppression by the Roman rulers took their toll on the Jewish people. The message of Jesus and his disciples seemed to offer hope to many disillusioned and poor Jews. Eventually, Judaism and Christianity split into two separate religions. Hostility, persecution, and mistrust between the two groups continued for centuries.

### Core Concepts

- Christianity's roots are in Judaism. The early Christians followed Jewish law yet they believed that Jesus was the Messiah.
- As Christianity became a separate religion, the seeds of mistrust, rivalry and persecution between Jews and Christians were sown.
- The world could become a better, more peaceful place by improving interfaith relations.

### Discussion Questions

1. What were the similarities and differences between early Christianity and Judaism? What are some of the core values that are still shared by Judaism and Christianity? What are some similarities between traditions that are practiced by Christian and Jewish communities today?

2. How does remembering that the Gospels were written before Christianity had split from Judaism and that most of the authors were Jewish help us to better understand the arguments and criticisms recorded in the Gospels?

3. Describe ways that interfaith relations in North America today can be improved. What are some of the greatest challenges? Can you identify programs within your community that promote understanding between people of different faiths?

# Chapter 6: Babylonia

***...book pages 57-66***

## *The New Center of Jewish Life*

### Chapter Overview

With the Jewish population concentrated in Babylonia, the impact of the Diaspora on Judaism grew. Judaism evolved as Jews were influenced by Babylonian culture and met the challenges of strengthening Jewish life. The Jews of this period not only developed the Babylonian Talmud, they also created a dynamic model for living as a minority in a non-Jewish environment.

### Core Concepts

- After the destruction of the Second Temple, Judaism continued to evolve as the Jewish people in the lands of the Diaspora found ways to adapt Jewish tradition (e.g. worshipping God without a Holy Temple) and integrate aspects of the surrounding cultures.
- To this day, the majority of Jews live outside of Israel, and the Diaspora remains a major spiritual and creative force in Jewish life.

**Words to Know**
*Talmud*: p.58. A compilation of Jewish law, tradition, stories, and commentary on the Bible.

### Discussion Questions

1. What were some of the greatest challenges Babylonian Jews faced because of the surrounding culture? How did they meet those challenges? What are some of the challenges Diaspora Jews today face because of their surrounding cultures? How do Jews today respond to these challenges while trying to maintain their Jewish identity?

2. What was the influence of the Talmud and its commentaries on Judaism? Why are most Jews today considered rabbinic Jews?

# Chapter 7: Sepharad and Ashkenaz

*...book pages 67-78*

## *Judaism's Increasing Diversity*

**Chapter Overview**

Many Jews left Babylonia for lands that are now known as Spain and Germany. The Jews of Spain, the Sephardic community, flourished under Muslim rule as they worked side by side with their Muslim and Christian neighbors. The Jews of Germany, the Ashkenazic community, did not have the same kinds of social and cultural relationships with non-Jews. Some of Judaism's greatest literary and theological works came from each of these communities.

**Core Concepts**

- The Diaspora broadened when the Jews left Babylonia and settled in new places.
- The Jewish communities of Spain and Germany developed in distinctive ways, yet they continued to share key traditions based on a belief in the sanctity of the Torah and a love for the Land of Israel.
- Today's Jewish communities are diverse yet continue to share the same core traditions and values.

| **Words to Know** |
|---|
| *Kabbalah*: p.69. Teachings of the Jewish mystics. |

**Discussion Questions**

1. Judah Halevi was a great Spanish Jewish poet, philosopher, physician, and merchant. Yet he longed for and eventually moved to the Land of Israel. Why might he have left all that he had to live in the Land of Israel? Why do some successful Jews today choose to make *aliyah* (immigrate to Israel) rather than remain in other countries?

2. How did integration or lack of integration into the surrounding cultures affect Jewish thought and scholarship in Spain and Germany? How does Jewish integration in North America influence Jewish thought, publications, scholarship, and politics today?

3. How and why did the Sephardic and Ashkenazic communities develop their own distinct customs and traditions? How do these differences affect relationships between these communities even in our own day? How might shared beliefs and values help different communities to understand and respect one another?

# Chapter 8: Medieval Europe

***...book pages 79-88***

## *The Rise of Religious Persecution*

### Chapter Overview

Competition between Jewish and Christian merchants in medieval Europe led to restrictions that forced Jews out of trade. Anti-Jewish laws were passed that stripped Jews of their freedom and imposed high taxes upon them. Persecution of the Jews grew as the Crusades stirred up local populations against non-Christians.

### Core Concepts

- Due to religious prejudice, political factors, and economic competition, the Jews became targets of persecution and violence in medieval Europe.
- Many forms of prejudice continue to plague our world. The world community is responsible for fighting against prejudice.

### Discussion Questions

1. What factors contributed to hideous accusations, such as blood libel, being unfairly leveled against the Jews? What are examples of religious or ethnic groups today being unfairly accused of crimes they have not committed? What can the world community do to fight against these false accusations?

2. Why was the Inquisition established? Why were new Christians who had recently converted from Judaism sometimes the most zealous inquisitors of the Jewish community? How can we lessen tensions today between people of one faith and those who have chosen to leave that faith for another?

3. How did Christian attitudes toward Jews contribute to many Jews becoming moneylenders? How do prejudices against ethnic, religious, and cultural groups influence professional opportunities in North America today? What is and can be done to insure greater opportunities for minority groups?

# Chapter 9: The Sephardic Diaspora

*...book pages 89-100*

## *Rebuilding Jewish Life*

### Chapter Overview

The Sephardic Jews, expelled from Spain, spread out in many directions and built new Jewish communities from Asia to the Americas. They enriched Judaism by producing works on Jewish law, by developing the Ladino language, and by creating the foundation of a Jewish community in North America. This was also a period of upheaval, a period when, in their search for hope, many Jews believed in false messiahs.

### Core Concepts

As a result of the Sephardic community's expulsion from Spain, Jews learned to:

- Never take their security for granted.
- Value the ties that unite all Jews no matter what their differences.
- Be flexible and adaptable.

**Words to Know**
*Tikun olam* ("repair the world"): p.94. Acts of social justice that make the world a better place.

### Discussion Questions

1. Why did some Spanish Jews practice Judaism in secret in the late 1300s and 1400s? How were these crypto-Jews similar to the Russian Jews who conducted underground seders during the 1980s? Today Jewish students and tourists who visit Arab countries are advised not to reveal their religion. How would you respond if you were told to hide your religious affiliation?

2. What were the values and ideals of the kabbalists in Safed? What are some examples of *tikun olam*, and how can participating in these acts of social justice create bonds among diverse groups of Jews? What role does Kabbalah play in North America today?

# Part Two Overview Questions ***...book pages 37-100***

These questions may be used to guide your discussions about the entirety of **Part Two: Diaspora and Diversity** (chapters 4-9).

1. What factors caused the Jews of Ashkenaz and the Jews of Sepharad to develop their own unique customs and traditions? How was each group shaped by its surrounding cultural, political, and religious environments? Which core values and beliefs shared by these two groups can help the two communities today to respect and understand each other?

2. What were some of the greatest challenges faced by Jewish communities in the Middle Ages? How did the communities respond to these challenges in order to keep Judaism thriving and vital? What can we learn from these communities about how to respond to challenges that threaten freedom of religion?

3. How did the Jews manage to keep Judaism alive and vigorous despite the destruction of the Second Temple and the shift of Jewish population from the Land of Israel to the Diaspora? How has modern Judaism been shaped by these adaptations?

4. What factors contributed to the hostility, persecution, and mistrust between Christians and Jews during the Middle Ages? How can we work today to lessen these conflicts and to strengthen positive interfaith relations?

# PART THREE: ENLIGHTENMENT AND EMANCIPATION

Jewish communities increasingly began to integrate into the societies around them as emancipation spread. Jews strived to adapt Judaism to the modern world without losing their core Jewish values.

## Chapter 10: The Polish Kehillah and German Enlightenment

*...book pages 103-114*

*Isolation Versus Integration*

### Chapter Overview

The ghettos of Poland and Lithuania segregated the Jews from their neighbors. The Jewish Enlightenment (Haskalah) paved the way for Jews to become integrated into modern society by making it possible for Jews to live and work with their non-Jewish neighbors.

### Core Concepts

- Judaism has often straddled the line between isolation and integration—maintaining close ties within the Jewish community and interacting with the broader community.
- Both approaches have helped to enrich Judaism and have led to diversity.

### Discussion Questions

1. How were the Jewish communities of Poland and Lithuania affected by their segregation from non-Jews? Why do you think some religious groups today choose to live in isolation from their surrounding communities? What are the benefits and consequences of living in an isolated community?

2. What factors contributed to the development of the Ḥasidim, the Mitnagdim, and the Maskilim? How have each group's values and teachings continued to influence Judaism to this day?

# Chapter 11: Revolution and Emancipation

*The Challenge of Freedom* *...book pages 115-122*

### Chapter Overview

Before emancipation, Jews often were forced to live separately from their non-Jewish neighbors. In these segregated communities, Jews were expected to follow Jewish law and tradition. The American and French Revolutions brought freedom to the Jews, which resulted in increased assimilation. As the ideas and spirit of the American and French Revolutions spread through Western Europe, so did emancipation. In Poland and Russia, life improved for the Jews, but formal emancipation did not come until the twentieth century.

### Core Concepts

- After emancipation, Jews no longer were required to be members of the Jewish community or to participate in Jewish communal life.
- In modern democratic countries Jews may choose to identify and live as Jews, or not, and this fact continues to shape Judaism.

**Words to Know**
*Emancipation*: p.115. Political freedom that enabled Jews to become full-fledged citizens of their countries.

### Discussion Questions

1. What effect did emancipation have on the role of the Jewish calendar in the lives of the French Jews? How and why do many Jews today continue to follow the Jewish calendar along with the secular calendar? In what other ways do North American Jews today have dual identities as Jews and citizens of their countries?

2. Compare Jewish life before and after emancipation. How have Judaism and the Jewish community been both strengthened and weakened by Jews achieving the full rights of citizens of the countries in which they live?

# Chapter 12: Judaism and the Modern World

*Finding a Balance* ***...book pages 123-134***

## Chapter Overview

Jews entered the middle class in major cities in England, Germany, Russia, and Poland, where they were encouraged to assimilate. Seeking to prove that they could be good citizens, many Jews struggled to adapt Judaism and Jewish identity to the modern world. This fostered the rise of different movements within Judaism, the forerunners of today's Reform, Conservative, and Orthodox movements.

## Core Concepts

- In order to maintain their Jewish identities, emancipated Jews either had to reject modern culture or adapt Judaism. Their choices led to greater diversity among the Jews.
- Today Jews continue to have diverse responses to the challenges and opportunities presented to them.

## Discussion Questions

1. How did German Jews respond to the German attitude that Jews were unfit for citizenship? How might you respond if you were told that you would not make a worthy citizen because of your religious affiliation?

2. What social and political influences in nineteenth-century Germany caused Judaism to begin to divide into Reform, Conservative, Modern Orthodox, and ultra-Orthodox Judaism? How do these different directions continue to influence Jews today?

3. Why did early Reform Judaism drop references to the Jews returning to the Land of Israel? The new Reform prayer book, *Mishkan T'filah*, includes prayers that affirm the movement's devotion to the modern State of Israel. What influences may have contributed to these prayers being included? How might the reinstatement of these prayers affect the ties between Reform Jews and Israel?

# Chapter 13: The Rise of Antisemitism ***...book pages 135-140***

## *Nationalism and the Search for Scapegoats*

### Chapter Overview

Anti-Jewish prejudice lingered on despite the legal gains of emancipation and the social gains of assimilation. A rise in nationalism in European countries heightened this antisemitism and caused people to question whether Jews were loyal citizens. Some more assimilated Jews began losing pride in their Jewish identity and were embarrassed by newly arrived Eastern European Jews who had not yet assimilated.

### Core Concepts

- Prejudice cannot be completely erased by legal mandates or a group's effort to assimilate into the larger society.
- The harm antisemitism does includes undermining Jewish identity and pride.

| **Words to Know** |
|---|
| *Chauvinism*: p.136. Extreme nationalism that inspires feelings of superiority. |

### Discussion Questions

1. What were the effects of extreme nationalism on the nineteenth-century European Jews? How does chauvinism remain a problem in North America today? How can we respond to it?

2. What factors contributed to the rise of antisemitism in nineteenth-century Europe? How is antisemitism in North America today similar to or different from that of nineteenth-century Europe? How can both Jews and non-Jews fight antisemitism, racism, and all forms of prejudice?

3. Why would antisemitism cause Jews to doubt themselves and judge each other? How did this self-doubt lead Central and Western European Jews to look down on Eastern European Jews who seemed to fit the antisemitic stereotype? What were and are the consequences of Jews looking down upon other Jews? How can this problem be addressed?

# Chapter 14: U.S. Jewry, 1820–1880 ***...book pages 141-152***

*Balancing Freedom with Tradition*

## Chapter Overview

The United States provided new opportunities for Judaism and Jewish communities to thrive. As Jews spread out across the United States and experienced the freedom to create an American style of Judaism, the Jewish religion and culture became increasingly diverse. Some Jews chose to completely assimilate into the American culture. Reform Judaism became more innovative, the seeds of Conservative Judaism were sown, and revivalists sought to adapt Judaism to life in America while promoting a resurgence of Jewish learning and observance.

## Core Concepts

- Emancipation and economic opportunity led to greater diversity in the Jewish community.
- Early Jewish immigrants struggled to balance their modern lives with a commitment to traditional Jewish values.
- The need to balance modernization and traditional Jewish values continues to stimulate change and creative adaptation in the Jewish community.

## Discussion Questions

1. What do you think Abraham Kohn meant when, describing the life of the Jewish peddler, he wrote, "Is such a life not enslavement rather than freedom?" Do you feel that you are free to rest from your work on the Sabbath? What considerations must be taken into account when one chooses not to work on the Sabbath in North America today? Is it possible to keep a religious life that adheres to the spirit but not the letter of the law? What does it mean to be authentically Jewish?

2. How did emancipation and economic opportunities shape the Jewish communities in nineteenth-century North America? How has your own family's choice of where to live been influenced by economic opportunities? What else has influenced where you have chosen to live?

3. What are some of the Jewish organizations that were born in North America in the 1800s? How do these different organizations continue to influence the Jewish community today?

# Part Three Overview Questions *...book pages 101-152*

These questions may be used to guide your discussions about the entirety of **Part Three: Enlightenment and Emancipation** (chapters 10-14).

1. From the 1500s through the 1800s Jews experienced segregation, integration, emancipation, and antisemitism. How were each of these—even emancipation, which should have been solely a positive force—a threat to the vitality of Judaism? How did the Jewish people adapt to each of these experiences as they maintained their core Jewish values? How do these adaptations continue to influence Judaism today?

2. How did the Haskalah, the Jewish Enlightenment, lead the way toward greater diversity in Jewish thought and practice? What shaped Reform, Conservative, Modern Orthodox, and ultra-Orthodox Judaism? How do these movements differ from one another? What core values do they share?

3. Why did Reform Jews in the 1800s break off their connection to the Land of Israel? How did the Reform position reflect the view that Jews are not a separate people or nation but only adherents of the Jewish religion? Why do you think that despite centuries of living in the Diaspora, Jews continued to hope for an independent state in their ancestral homeland?

# PART FOUR: ANTISEMITISM AND ZIONISM

The rise of antisemitism made it difficult for Jews to adapt to their surrounding cultures and also contributed to dreams of a Jewish state.

## Chapter 15: Eastern European Jewry, 1881–1914

*Turmoil and Transformation* ***...book pages 155-160***

**Chapter Overview**

After the assassination of Czar Alexander II, life changed for the worse for the Jews of Russia. Jews were motivated by anti-Jewish policies, riots, and pogroms to find ways to survive and to improve their lives. Many stayed in Russia and worked to improve conditions there, some immigrated to the Land of Israel, and others moved to South Africa, Argentina, and North America.

**Core Concepts**

- Russian and European Jews responded to the unfulfilled hopes of emancipation with diverse strategies. Some stayed in their countries and combined Jewish values with Socialism, others immigrated to Palestine, and yet others moved to more emancipated lands in the Diaspora.
- Jews continue to seek diverse solutions to maintaining their freedom and their Jewish identities.

**Discussion Questions**

1. What were some of the challenges faced by Jews living under Czars Alexander III and Nicholas II? In what ways did Jewish life change under czarist rule? How did the antisemitic forgery *The Protocols of the Elders of Zion* contribute to antisemitism? How does it still contribute to antisemitism?

2. What political and economic factors led to the creation of the Bund? Which Jewish values and ideals shaped this group? How do these values and ideals continue to influence the Jewish community today?

3. How was the movement among Eastern European Jews to revive Hebrew as a national language connected to their hope to return to Palestine (the Land of Israel)? How and why did the choice to write in Hebrew versus Yiddish create conflicts among Eastern European Jews? How can learning modern Hebrew help Diaspora Jews strengthen their ties to the State of Israel?

# Chapter 16: The Great Migration

*...book pages 161-168*

## *New Challenges to Jewish Tradition*

### Chapter Overview

Seeking a better life, hundreds of thousands of Jews immigrated to the United States from Eastern Europe and Russia. The new arrivals moved to Jewish communities where housing and places of work were often overcrowded, unsanitary, and hazardous. In response to those conditions, Jews established labor unions and other organizations to better the lives of the new immigrants.

### Core Concepts

- The majority of the two million Russian and European Jews who immigrated to the United States both adapted to their surroundings *and* maintained their Jewish identities.
- The Jewish values of social justice and community inspired the new immigrants to fight for better lives for themselves and for all Americans.
- Today, Jews continue to be faced with the challenge of maintaining their Jewish identities as they work with others in support of social justice for all people.

### Discussion Questions

1. What were some of the social and economic challenges faced by Jews who immigrated to the United States in the late 1800s and early 1900s? How did the Jewish value of social justice influence Jews to work toward improving the new immigrants' living and working conditions? What can we do today to help improve living and working conditions for new immigrants both in North America and in Israel?

2. Why did so many Jews leave Europe for the United States between 1900 and 1914? When and why did your family first come to North America? How has your family adapted to life in North America since your ancestors first immigrated here?

# Chapter 17: Jewish Nationalism and Zionism

*Imagining a Modern Jewish State* ***...book pages 169-178***

## Chapter Overview

A wave of nationalism in Europe, coupled with the impact of antisemitism and deadly pogroms, set the stage for Zionism. Thousands of Russian and Eastern European Jews began to immigrate to Palestine in hopes of building the Jewish homeland. Western European Jews were less interested in Zionism because emancipation had been much more successful in their countries. To this day, most new immigrants to Israel come from lands in which Jews have been oppressed.

## Core Concepts

- With the rise of nationalism and increased antisemitism in Europe, many Jews turned to Zionism as a source of hope.
- Early Zionists had diverse beliefs regarding where the Jewish state should be and what it should be like.
- Today, Jews continue to have diverse views regarding the Jewish state.

**Words to Know**
*Zionism*: p.172. The movement to establish and support a modern Jewish state in the Land of Israel.

## Discussion Questions

1. Inspired by the rise of nationalism, some Jews became Jewish nationalists. What is the difference between thinking about Judaism as a *religion* and thinking about Judaism as a *nation*? How do you think about your own identity?

2. What roles did antisemitism and Jewish nationalism play in motivating Jews to immigrate to the Land of Israel during the First and Second Aliyah movements? What were the challenges, failures, and successes of each wave of immigration? What values, ideals,and life situations motivate Jews today to immigrate to Israel?

3. Read an English translation of "Hatikvah" ("The Hope"). How do the words of this song reflect the ideals, hopes, and emotions of the early Zionists? Do you think that "Hatikvah," which was formally named the State of Israel's national anthem in 2004, continues to express the thoughts and feelings of Jews today? Why or why not?

# Chapter 18: World War I

***...book pages 179-186***

## *Reaching Out Across the Diaspora*

### Chapter Overview

During World War I, Jews fought against other Jews as they joined their nations' armies. After the war, the Jews of Eastern Europe and Russia suffered from poverty and a rise in antisemitism. Other Diaspora Jews joined together to provide support for Eastern European and Russian Jewry. Simultaneously, Diaspora Jews worked toward the establishment of a Jewish state.

### Core Concepts

- During World War I, Jews were caught on both sides of the largest and deadliest war the world had ever known.
- The center of Jewish life began to shift after World War I from Eastern Europe to the United States and the Land of Israel.
- After the war, Jews of different backgrounds joined together to help Jews throughout the Diaspora. The American Jewish community continues to play an important role in supporting Diaspora communities and the modern State of Israel.

### Discussion Questions

1. How did the desire to show loyalty to one's nation motivate Jews to fight in World War I? To what degree did relations between Jews and non-Jews improve after they fought together in the war? Do you think the desire to demonstrate loyalty to one's homeland continues to motivate Diaspora Jews to be part of the armed forces?

2. What were some of the effects of World War I on various Jewish communities? How is the American Joint Distribution Committee an outstanding example of diverse groups of Jews coming together for a single purpose? "The Joint" still remains an important organization. What were some of its original concerns? Which major issues do you think it should address today?

3. How and why did early twentieth-century Diaspora Jews contribute to the Zionist movement? Why was Louis Brandeis so influential among Jews? Whom do you see as positive Jewish role models today? What have they done or what issues do they support? What role does being Jewish play in their lives?

# Chapter 19: At Home in the United States, 1920–1940

## *Creating an American Style of Judaism* 

***...book pages 187-196***

### Chapter Overview

After the Immigration Act of 1924, which limited the number of immigrants from Eastern and Southern Europe into the United States, native-born American Jews outnumbered the immigrant Jewish population. The face of Judaism changed as Jews born in America adapted to their new home: bat mitzvah ceremonies were introduced, many Jews became more secular and less religiously observant, and synagogues developed into community centers.

### Core Concepts

- As native-born American Jews began to outnumber the immigrant Jewish population, Jews became integrated into American society.
- Many Jews maintained a strong Jewish identity that was based largely on ethnic ties rather than on religious principles.
- During this period a uniquely American style of Judaism began to develop, helping to shape today's Jewish community.

### Discussion Questions

1. What conditions contributed to antisemitism in America in the 1920s and 1930s? How did Jews respond to antisemitism during this period? What is the significance of changing one's name? If your family name has been changed, why was it changed? What do you think the effect is today of having a Jewish sounding name?

2. Why and how did Reform, Conservative, and Orthodox Judaism develop in America during the 1920s and 1930s? What were some of their key differences? How were they influenced by Reconstructionism? What core values were, and are, shared by these diverse groups?

3. In what ways did some Jews connect to Judaism more as a cultural identity than a religious identity as they adapted to middle-class life in America? How did Jewish leaders respond to the challenge of making Judaism more meaningful to American Jews? What are the advantages and disadvantages of an identity based on ethnic ties rather than religious beliefs?

# Chapter 20: The British Mandate ...*book pages 197-206*

## *Zionist Achievements and Arab-Israeli Conflict*

### Chapter Overview

Both Jews and Arabs celebrated when the British defeated the Turks and took control of Palestine. But it did not take long for tensions to escalate between the two groups, both of whom wanted control over the same small piece of land. The Jews of Palestine formed an illegal underground militia to protect themselves against attacks by Arabs. In response to growing conflicts, the British limited Jewish immigration to Palestine and land sales to Jews in Palestine. The seeds of the Arab-Jewish conflict were sown during this period.

### Core Concepts

- This was a time of great growth and achievement for the Zionists of Palestine.
- A new image of the Jew as a courageous and powerful pioneer and soldier was emerging.
- During this period, seeds of conflict between the Jews and Arabs were sown.

**Words to Know**
*Yishuv* ("settlement"): pp.176, 199. The Jewish community of Palestine before the establishment of the State of Israel.

### Discussion Questions

1. What factors led the British to withdraw the promises they had made to the Jews in the Balfour Declaration, as well as the promises they had made to the Arabs before the defeat of the Turks? What were the ramifications of the White Paper? How do these decisions continue to affect Jews and Arabs today?

2. How was the image of the early Yishuv settlers, the *ḥalutzim*, different from that of the Eastern European Jews? What contributions were made by the settlers as they worked to build a modern homeland for the Jews? How are the ideals the *ḥalutzim* brought to Palestine (Hebrew language, self-defense, and social justice) apparent in the State of Israel today?

3. Why did the leaders of the Yishuv decide not to cooperate with the British in Palestine, but to fight alongside the British against Hitler? Do you think this was a valid political position? Are there situations today in which you support a government's position on one issue but disagree with it in regard to another?

# Chapter 21: Europe Between the Wars ***...book pages 207-214***

## *Rising Antisemitism and Jewish Diversity*

### Chapter Overview

After World War I, many European Jews were still viewed as outsiders in their home countries. Jews generally responded to this antisemitism in four different ways: living and working separately from non-Jews, attempting to integrate into the larger secular culture, returning to the Jewish homeland, or supporting Socialism and Communism. All four solutions failed to keep the Jews safe as economic depression spread and Adolf Hitler rose to power in Germany.

### Core Concepts

- Emancipation allowed Western European Jews to assimilate into secular culture to a greater extent than the Eastern European Jews could.
- Jews developed diverse responses to the challenge of antisemitism: remaining separate, assimilating, returning to the Land of Israel, and supporting revolutionary change.
- Social, economic, and political freedoms continue to pose challenges today to Jewish identity and commitment to Judaism.

### Discussion Questions

1. How and why did four separate responses to antisemitism develop among European Jews in the 1920s? Imagine being a Jew in Europe during this era. How might you have responded? Why?

2. What cultural and scientific contributions did European Jews of the 1920s make despite the rise of antisemitism? How do these contributions to society continue to influence Jews and non-Jews today?

3. What lessons can be learned about stopping evil before it gets out of hand by looking at Hitler's rise to power? How can we respond to the fact that Hitler seized power democratically, in a nationwide election?

# Part Four Overview Questions ***...book pages 153-214***

These questions may be used to guide your discussions about the entirety of **Part Four: Antisemitism and Zionism** (chapters 15-21).

1. How did the face of world Jewry change from the 1880s to the 1930s? What motivated some Jews to move to the Land of Israel or North America, while others chose to remain in Western or Eastern Europe? How and why did Judaism evolve into four different movements in North America? How do the changes during this period impact on Jews today?

2. What social and political factors set the stage for Zionism? Describe some of the beliefs regarding what the Jewish state should be like. Which of these early visions of a Jewish state are evidenced in the modern State of Israel?

3. How did the Jewish value of *tikun olam*, social justice, influence Jews to work to improve the societies in which they lived? What were some of the ways Jews adapted to European and American cultures? How did the rise of antisemitism make it difficult for Jews to adapt to their surrounding cultures? How do North American Jews today balance Jewish identity with secular identity?

# Part Five: Devastation and Rebirth

The Holocaust brought devastation on a scale never before imagined. In the aftermath, the Zionist dream of a Jewish state finally became reality, but not without significant new challenges.

## Chapter 22: The Holocaust

*...book pages 217-226*

*The Monstrous Cost of Intolerance and Indifference*

**Chapter Overview**

Under Hitler's Nazi party, Germany conquered most of Europe and ruthlessly murdered at least six million Jews. After many centuries of vibrant Jewish life there, Europe was no longer the spiritual and population center of world Jewry. Many of the roughly three million surviving European Jews immigrated to the United States and Canada at the end of World War II. Some, convinced that the Jewish future lay in the Land of Israel, chose to live in Palestine.

**Core Concepts**

- Violent antisemitism combined with moral indifference toward the suffering of others allowed Hitler to carry out his plans against the European Jews.
- Jews organized underground operations and joined the Allied Powers' armed forces in an effort to resist the Nazi onslaught.
- Putting their own lives at risk, courageous non-Jews saved the lives of thousands of Jews.

**Discussion Questions**

1. How did antisemitism outside Europe prevent Jews from leaving Europe and contribute to Hitler's design of the "final solution"? What lessons should the world community have learned from the Holocaust in regard to combating atrocities such as the violence in Darfur? What are some examples of Jewish organizations today being proactive in fighting for justice and human rights?

2. How did both Jews and non-Jews oppose the Nazis? What risks did these courageous people take? What do you think gives someone the courage to risk his or her own life to fight against injustice in hopes of saving others?

# Chapter 23: The Birth of the Modern State of Israel

*From Dream to Reality* ***...book pages 227-236***

## Chapter Overview

Unable to resolve the tensions and fighting between the Arabs and Jews of Palestine, the British handed the problem over to the United Nations. The UN devised a partition plan, dividing Palestine into two states that no longer would be ruled by the British: one Arab and one Jewish. The new Jewish state was immediately met by the challenges of war, hostile neighbors, and the absorption of hundreds of thousands of poor Jewish immigrants.

## Core Concepts

- The Arabs did not accept partition, and immediately after the establishment of the Jewish state, Arab armies invaded Israel.
- After the War of Independence, Israel was faced with the challenge of absorbing a flood of new Jewish immigrants.
- The achievements of Israeli Jews often add to the pride Diaspora Jews feel in their own Jewish identities.

## Discussion Questions

1. How did the assistance given by the Jews of Palestine and America to the survivors of the Holocaust exemplify the Jewish value of *Kol Yisrael areivim zeh ba-zeh*, all Israel is responsible for one another? In what ways do Jews today continue to uphold this core value?

2. The establishment of the State of Israel created the opportunity for unlimited Jewish immigration to Israel. How did this policy affect Jews all over the world? Is this policy still important today?

3. What were some of the challenges faced by Middle Eastern and North African Jews who immigrated to Israel? How are these challenges similar to those faced by immigrants to America or Israel today? What can be done to help immigrants be absorbed into a new country?

# Chapter 24: Making It in America, 1945–1965

## *Golden Decades*

***...book pages 237-246***

### Chapter Overview

The years 1945 through 1965 are sometimes referred to as the Golden Decades in American Jewish history. As antisemitism declined and the economy grew, it became easier for Jews to gain admittance into colleges, get better jobs, and buy homes in the suburbs. During this time, Jewish identity remained strong, and record numbers of Jews joined synagogues and sent their children to religious schools. Jews became political and civil rights activists as expressions of both their American and their Jewish identities.

### Core Concepts

- While Jews were joining synagogues in record numbers, many were drawn to the social rather than the religious aspects of synagogue life.
- Many Jews became social and political activists in the 1960s, as liberal rabbis increasingly promoted prophetic Judaism, the ethical teachings of the Hebrew prophets.
- As Jews have been accepted into mainstream American life and culture, their American identities have been strengthened. This has both enriched and challenged their Jewish identities.

### Discussion Questions

1. What factors motivated many Jews to move from cities to suburbs? How did this change in demographics affect Judaism in America? How does Judaism today continue to be influenced by the changes that took place from 1945 to 1965?

2. What were some of the causes for which Jews were motivated to fight? In what ways do you agree, or disagree, with Abraham Joshua Heschel's statement, "The opposite of good is not evil. The opposite of good is indifference"? In your opinion, what shapes and prepares a person to fight for social justice?

# Chapter 25: The Diaspora Consolidates

## *A Shrinking Jewish World*

***...book pages 247-254***

### Chapter Overview

Prior to World War II, Jews lived on six continents. The rise of antisemitism in many countries spurred millions of Jews to leave their homes and immigrate to Israel, the United States, and Canada. As a result, Judaism changed from a world religion to a regional religion centered in the world's wealthiest and most advanced countries.

### Core Concepts

- Since the end of World War II, millions of Jews have migrated from underdeveloped, unstable, and dangerous countries to economically affluent, politically stable, and socially attractive ones.
- Due to this shift in population, Jews live in fewer countries around the world, and most of the world outside these major Jewish communities no longer has firsthand knowledge of Jews and Judaism.

### Discussion Questions

1. Since the end of World War II, what political, economic, and social factors have motivated Jews to immigrate to Israel and America? What are the positive and negative effects of having most of the world's Jewish population living in just two countries?

2. What were some of the challenges faced by Soviet Jews? How were the Jews of Israel and the United States able to pressure the Soviet Union to allow Jews to emigrate from there? What can we learn from the actions of the Soviet Jews and the Diaspora Jews who acted on their behalf?

3. How did the schools established by the Alliance Israélite Universelle in North Africa and Iran help prepare the Jews for the modern world? What losses may have occurred through this approach? How can people best be absorbed into society yet maintain their own cultural identity?

# Chapter 26: Israel in Our Time

*...book pages 255-264*

## *An Ongoing Story of Challenge and Triumph*

### Chapter Overview

The diversity of the Israeli population—rich and poor, religious and secular, Jewish, Muslim, and Christian—is both a challenge and a blessing to the State of Israel. The one challenge that has dominated all others, however, is the conflict with the Palestinians and surrounding Arab countries. Since its founding, Israel has often been at war with its Arab neighbors, yet it continues to work with its allies and its enemies to establish a lasting peace.

### Core Concepts

- The diversity of the Israeli population has brought many challenges, including the uneasy balance between religious and secular influences, and the growing gap between wealthy and poor people.
- At times, Israel has successfully negotiated peace treaties with its enemies. In other cases, attempts at negotiations have ended in failure and bloodshed.
- Pursuing peace is a basic Jewish value. The Jewish people have the responsibility to support efforts to bring peace to Israel.

**Words to Know**

*Intifada* ("shaking off"): p.261. The Palestinian uprising against Israel that began in 1987 in Gaza and the West Bank.

### Discussion Questions

1. Why does Israel today have such a diverse Jewish population? What are some of the challenges faced by different segments of the population? What values and beliefs are shared by most Israeli Jews?

2. What problems were created between Jews and Arabs as a result of the Six-Day War? What are some of the efforts that have been made to resolve these conflicts? What remain some of the greatest obstacles to achieving peace in the State of Israel? How might peace be attained?

3. How do religious and secular Jews in Israel disagree on the meaning of a "Jewish state"? What does it mean to non-Jewish Israelis? How might the State of Israel find a balance between these differing opinions?

# Chapter 27: American Jewry Today *...book pages 265-275*

## *Making the Choice to Survive and Thrive*

### Chapter Overview

Living in North America has given Jews the opportunity to freely practice Judaism and choose how to lead Jewish lives. Issues related to Israel, social activism, feminism, and gay and lesbian rights are among the many concerns that have shaped the Jewish identities of North American Jews. Today, Jews in North America enjoy the advantages of religious freedom but also face challenges to the future of Judaism.

### Core Concepts

- The American Jewish community has continually responded to changing conditions and opportunities by adapting in diverse and creative ways.
- Jews in North America today are confronted with the challenges of intermarriage, assimilation, and decreased birth rates.
- Today's young people will write the next chapter of Jewish history in North America, through the lives they live and the choices they make.

### Discussion Questions

1. What kind of relationship has existed between American Jews and Israel since the 1960s? What challenges does this relationship face today? What can be done to strengthen the connections between Israeli and American Jews?

2. How has the feminist movement influenced the role of women in Judaism? How do changes, such as women becoming clergy and being counted in a minyan, affect the Jewish community as a whole?

3. What are some of the ways that Jews have adapted to living in America while maintaining their Jewish identity and Jewish values? What are some of the challenges the American Jewish community will most likely face in the upcoming years? How can American Jews respond to these challenges and maintain a strong Jewish community?

# Part Five Overview Questions

*...book pages 215-275*

These questions may be used to guide your discussions about the entirety of **Part Five: Devastation and Rebirth** (chapters 22-27).

1. Why has the Jewish population shifted from being spread across six continents to being largely located in North America and Israel? How have Jews adapted to new living situations after emigrating from their homelands? What have been some of the greatest challenges and how have they been met? Based on these demographic changes, what challenges do you foresee in the future and how can they be addressed?

2. How have both America and Israel developed a great diversity in their Jewish populations? What are some of the different groups that comprise the American Jewish community and Israeli society? What core values and beliefs are shared by all these groups?

3. What role has Israel played for the worldwide Jewish community since the end of World War II? How do events in Israel affect Diaspora Jews? Why is it important that Jews around the world maintain a close relationship with Israel and Israeli Jews? What can be done to foster positive relations between Diaspora Jews and Israel?